I0807238

COMMON WEALTH

D.A. LOCKHART

KEGEDONCE PRESS, 2025

Copyright © by D.A. Lockhart.
February 2025

Published by Kegedonce Press
11 Park Road, Neyaashiinigmiing, ON N0H 2T0
Administration Office/Book Orders: P.O. Box 517, Owen Sound, ON N4K 5R1
www.kegedonce.com

Printed in Canada by Gilmore Printing Services Inc.
Copy Editor: Richard-Yves Sitoski
Art Direction: Kateri Akiwenzie-Damm
Design: Chantal Lalonde Design
Author's photo: D.A. Lockhart

Library and Archives Canada Cataloguing in Publication

Title: Commonwealth / D.A. Lockhart.
Names: Lockhart, D. A., 1976- author
Identifiers: Canadiana 20240536649 | ISBN 9781928120483 (softcover)
Subjects: LCGFT: Poetry.
Classification: LCC PS8623.O295 C66 2025 | DDC C811/.6—dc23

All rights reserved. No part of this book may be reproduced in any form or by any electronic or mechanical means including information storage and retrieval systems, without permission in writing from the Publisher. Member of Access Copyright Sales and Distribution – www.litdistco.ca

For Customer Service/Orders
Tel 1-800-591-6250 Fax 1-800-591-6251
100 Armstrong Ave. Georgetown, ON L7G 5S4
Email: orders@litdistco.ca

We acknowledge the support of the Canada Council for the Arts which last year invested $20.1 million in writing and publishing throughout Canada.

Canada Council for the Arts | Conseil des arts du Canada

We would like to acknowledge funding support from the Ontario Arts Council, an agency of the Government of Ontario.

ONTARIO ARTS COUNCIL
CONSEIL DES ARTS DE L'ONTARIO
an Ontario government agency
un organisme du gouvernement de l'Ontario

For Benjamin Goluboff

CONTENTS

Mëkëkèkink

Anukanink

Kitutènay Shinkàskunk

Commonwealth

linkwehëleokàn yapei

i)

The land to the south of here is
called by its people a Commonwealth.
It is not our land. This earth beneath us
calls for roots, black earth. And the old
church reaches beneath, staring down
the Ohio as it passes, always moving,
always telling us there is life when we
fail to see it. We understand that our
kikayuyëmënaninka knew the hills,
the trickle of waters, the subtle shifts
between seasons, the manner earth
beneath them breathes, makes home.

Yukwe ènta kishkwik, this river before
me is our border against what was lost,
how it could come to be lost, and me here,
lost in thinking nkata kwsi, definite need
less than want, the river our model,
and the land across the way an apparition,
fading away in early morning fog, less
shadow than memory. What is common
holds no centre in this land nor there,
the bank opposite me and this church
lose their hard edges in this spring air.

Above the waters, the Good Waters,
I feel the gentle pull of earth to the north
of here. Whispers ìkalìchi nkata ktan.

ii)

Consider this loose union of humanity,
how it writhes against itself in strange
embrace. The pledges we make to each
other and we often fail to deliver upon
are bonds we use to hold to each other
in foreign lands. We hide from failures
in motion, both personal, structural.
We save ourselves from failures through
our motion, both are personal, structural.

Migration as failure of union.
Migration as completion of union.
Joined in flight, we are not alone.

In motion, we are wild spring rains
released across watersheds. Part damage,
part new life, a manner of balancing
wealth and commonly held earth,
yet it is in our beings to move.
This fog must break, we are not
ourselves when we are at rest.

The cost of staying far exceeds
the price of surviving. Common
calculations. All instinct, anxiety
in blood earned in violence, we must
pour north drawn in collective migration.

All land is transitory in the end,
even when held in treaty, even when
we define our words by it, even after
the final utterances tumble out onto
earth that shall never exist again.

iii)

Begin with how one builds words,
compounding. Stretch them over land
encompassing bluegrass hills, limestone
caves, meandering hollers, cranberry
marshes. We know of this place through
childhood tales spoke softly before sleep,
ahanhùkwi nuhëma whispered
from distance echoes of totemic
great grandparents. Tales of oft idyllic
lives offset by wars between aèsësàk.

Ahope, our closest utterance for wealth,
imported sense that meets our sense
of strength. The river is strong,
Ahopesipu. Rich, she churns with
that which these cradle lands left her.

Lenii the principal centre of our being,
the root ember of creator within
us all. Commonality a performance
of living. Leniiahope. A union
not through land, but rather essence.

I feel the listless breeze slide up
over the banks, lifting up kaòkche
towards the fog dulled sky. Close
enough there are tendrils, almost
visible and to the touch they are
cold like the river, yet kaòkche
rises, then pushes north, over the
hills and inland. River says it
again, ìkalìchi nkata ktan.

ÒSAOHANE

From Here Northward

You would not say every
home points north here.
Tight-packed to shoulder
width roads, you would say
they face each other,
look no further than
their neighbour, Eighth
street runs the length
of creation. Here is built
the vista of neighbours,
proximity of family, know
half of these houses are
empty in the way that
lets show the intent
is to always return here.

The Commonwealth giveth.
The Commonwealth taketh.
And the word heard most
about this place beyond
the river is migration.

In the passing warmth
of a spring sun on coffee
left exposed to sky, you feel
the anticipation of return
the same wafting earthiness
of freshly poured three-finger
bourbon wash, and then melt
river bronze into your being.

Outside Cincinnati

The county cut open before
me, serpentine highway runs
between, buildings, hillsides,
church spires, multitudes of
trees and parked cars. Beyond
road terminus, Ohio falls off
into its namesake river. Here
the interstate arrives like
afterthought, over-worn its
welcome. Slow crawl traffic
through sharp-edge debris
of past commutes gone wrong.

This is the manner we enter this
Queen City evening; constricted,
metal tang of exhaust, scanning
each hillside and every rooftop
for evidence that all before us
could have arisen from land
I know of through ancestral
blood echoes, long-quieted stories
of wars between mastodons
and the breadth of creation.

Upon these Levee-Shielded Streets

Here, to the boulevard
        behind levees and good sense
        to remain wholly commonwealth
        in spite of the Midwest beyond
        I walk, sight fixed to the river
        between misguided,
        under-appreciated academic
        roundtables on migration,
        the other, and all the things
red-hatted undesirables
fear in them. I am upon their

land. Signed away
        in treaty to unfaithful
        murderers. Let me believe
        lines such as these capable
        of taming the meanders
        of Kentucky, brick buildings,
        into daylight's meander of streets
        chiseled by the rebellions,
        carried by freight trains
        as they run atop us.

This Germanic river port
        town parades itself behind
        a Wild Turkey crucifix
        and the sure-fire approach
        of cranes, clearing a gentle
slope of land for parking garages

and head shops. Here, I find rest.
        Here, the South entreaties
        upon the ways the heartland
        pains you, the way that it needs
        you to be. Says you are all
        the good that you must be,
        history is something we survive

present is something we endure
in the rise of a changing
skyline, inflating real estate
the levee shall keep back
the worst. Our roots shall hold.

The Train Above 6th Street

I've heard these medicine songs
all my life: slow diesel grind
of graffiti-stained steel on rail,
shaking of walls, foundations.

This the song to quiet the wails
of feral cats, the mechanizing
rattle of dried leaves trapped
on last season's vines, fence posts.

Tonight, they sing me to sleep.
These double-railed slow grind songs
cutting distance between the shores
of Opèk Sipu, Waawiiyaatanong,
waters between us, and the viaduct
as it rolls past the Uptown mission,
trailing off into the dark hills above.

At Night I Breathe the Kentucky Air

Know that we build
homes, push roots
into the soil, in spite
of how
we feel we are
given to flight.

Migration the default.

Dreams arise from this default,
the parts we can't
switch off.
Vistas of three story tall
Appalachia successes
and train horns
calling into the night.

Even here, where the air
is sweet with mint,
wild, that never fails
to arrive in season,
lingers
well past its time.
I must fight the default.

Feel that this place is my past,
rectangular houses
clutched to roadsides,
resting along the wrong
bank of a fine river.

I shall move as occasion
rises,
wary that starting
still making you either
a tree or another
eroded shoreline.

Persistent, vivid dreams of what
    we can't be. At night,
    I breathe this Kentucky air.

Prayer Gathering at Zola Pub and Grill, Covington, Kentucky

Among these hills,
ramshackle triangle roads
witness the way homes
cling to the edges,
want eagerly for action
along these streets,
the ferocity of views
in the budding coffee
bean trees, the want
that cold be chased
away. Here, they smoke
indoors, from thirst
resolved with Yuengling
find passing destinations
in grapefruit league
on suspended televisions.

Where I-75 meets, then
runs over the great muddy
trans-territorial river, we
wait together in awe
of how tightly we cling
to what was given us,
lie in wait for what should
return, pray with each exhale
that we outlast those freeways
blasted through coal-lined hills.

Behind Greer Street Our Night Fills with Howls

Two cats face off
with night terror
howls behind Greer
Street, homes wreathed
in desiccate vines akin
to those climbing
viaduct walls behind.

Howls fill a night
between the passing
of freight trains,
oil cars aplenty,
and in the open door
to the gallery behind me,
Cincinnati fights against
a new moon softness
through two-turreted old
growth neighborhoods

Above viaduct tracks
in immaculate light
of Church spires, backlit
double crucifixes against
cold spring clouds
that threaten more rain
to muddy mean Ohio.

I shut the door, am left
with old man grumbles
of another passing train,
glass block windows quiet
atavistic feline battles,
domesticate this night
bracketed by the passions
of feral cats, and that
which cities fight against.

Week's End Arrives at Pike Street

I cascade towards sleep
with the white noise
of digital waves. Consider
the weight of Pelee even
this far south, know
that the trees have
fallen silent and Neutral
Sea waves have slowed,
evened into a crawl holler
of this settler town preened
at the Ohio River's divide.

Inland rail fences
give way to long
winter of detritus
plants unwilling to die
the persistent song
of wrens, shadows
of ever-present rats.

There is reason to believe
that in Covington, God
rests come Treaty night,
awakes only slightly
on Sunday and blesses
the survival of the week
with high-sin spring nights
and the winds that let you
know the recent has no place
with us. The bells are silent.

Sweet Ramen at Main Strasse, Covington, Kentucky

His complaint is about heat,
curses the ramen
and quiet
of exposed brick,
subway tile
and delivered in Yankee
cadence.

This bar, with us, waking up
late
and him still
determinedly shoveling noodles
and far too sweet broth
into his mouth.

In between slurps,
he proclaims
a disdain for this place;

a fair-weather shelter
against the day that
those around us felt
might never come.

Him, plagued by work,
disappointment
that wealth is that which
none of us can ever catch.

His actions, his meal
indications of his willingness
to do
what must be done.
To eat what does not
satisfy hunger,
limp
through another unwelcome day

of work, and do so
because rivers run,
sun rises, and the impossible
catch lies somewhere
beyond the next work shift,
and with the grace of God,
a little less sweet
than the broth
he slurps one last time
               wipes his mouth
               with shirt sleeve.

Weli Sipu

for the Ohio River

as if language
like land could
be held by any
factor beyond one's self-
deception; these waters
are welhik, the good ones,
that nurture, that provide,
that divide us from caves, hills,
meadows haunted by evil
medicines that scoured them
nkikayuyëmënaninkahke
from land they understood
is more than words
used to claim it.

Flows, curls to soft
shorelines, this river
holds many here.
Shawnuwàk held up here,
our relations.

Here a cradle of high water
caressed land. Faint touches
of deep Appalachian spirits
shimmering of thunderbeings
in the currents, water once
sweet carries past us
as it did then, does now.

Nkata Kwsi

Begin with want because want
empowers more than need, tell
all the truths about how needs
are the conditions we can't abide
without. Let that move you, push
you over borders, rivers, hills,
and hollers. We are more than
names and lines on wealthy men's
papers. Our wants emerge from
repressed needs, pathways across
the turtle shell world natural
to how we must wander like
sisilieyòk through traces scoured
by treaty and by black powder
metal shard threats. These lands
stolen by the few, impossibility
to hold back what comes naturally.

I want to move because borders
define both needs and wants,
and living by those alone ain't
living. And movement is life
beyond violence, in flight body
blows don't land, and the wind
is sweet in its perpetual coaxing.

Follow the arcing paths of night
heron, relentless trickle of rivers
emerging from their subterranean
aquifers, wind twitch of creation
reflected in midafternoon shadows.

AHCHUWIKEE

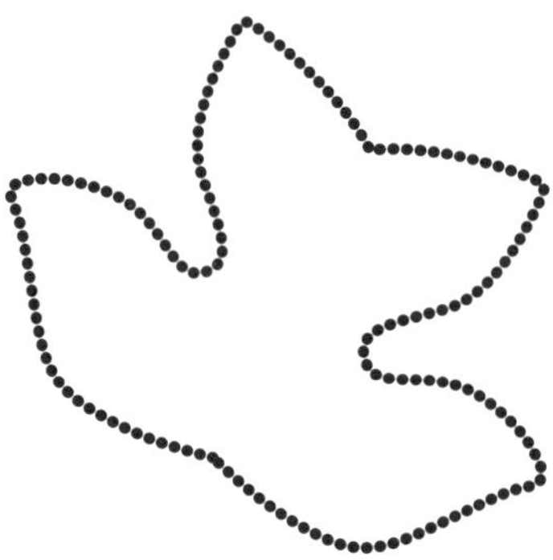

Across the Buffalo Trace

Through coal hummocks,
        sycamore lowlands,
        wildcat forests,
        the search
is for rolling waters,
        pathways to open skies,
        and the motion
        of it all.

In motion
        we are all
        truly saved
        and we cross
        the toes of land
        descending
        from Muncie.

Closer to earth than sun
we can trace earlier steps,
                Totemic sisilieyòk
                flatten ground,
                passages, long grooves
                between these hills,

etchings of free motions,
        of following richness like the sun.

And us East to West.
        wèhènchiopànk,
                where the bones we dance
                with were uprooted from.
        èhëliwsikakw
                where the trains once push,
                sisilieyòk drew near their last.

Yet from the Commonwealth
        we've always seen the path north.

from Palmyra through to Paoli
        shadows cling harder to road edges
        and on past French Lick,
        clear past Loogootee, you know
        better than to tumble
                with creek water
                down to the Wabash
                past Vincennes.

Certainly, it's the crush
        of those path carvers
        and insolvable weight against
        earth that cannot depart
        in human time that threatens

to carry
        everything with it
                into greater rivers
                                beyond
                                and the wide
                violent   sea   further still.

At Hindostan

Falls here are slight,
            an aberration of the gentle slide
            of waters downgrade. River onto
                                                river
is a whimper above the racket of trees.

And here the water ran to poison
                        and the town ran dry
            to the shores of the river.
And what remains,
            ever-quieting stories of tax collector
            buried treasure, a single sign, *1828*
                        bringing death to the inhabitants.
                                    The town was never occupied
                                                again.

Canned Cow Brains at Smokin' Jacks Rib Shack, Bloomington, Indiana

This cue like a chuckwagon
corral from WRTV
cowboys and Indians
Saturday nights, &
righteous Hoosier
men and women.

WRTV still broadcasting.
wild west phantoms long past.
And in the age, food remains.

Behold, the unspoken of commodity
outward facing to those in line.

Here it rests,
kitsch vintage
forty years of kitchen grease
adhered to smoothed
edges of bovine offal

Brain, canned the better
part of every lifetime ago.

And it stands defiant between
molasses heavy rib tips
in the rustic log house
of Appalachian road trips

and it dares,
unopened. Waiting.

My Rose of Old Kentucky Settles like Dew Across the Brown County Hills

In certainty, Bill Monroe sang
down this Brown County sun,
not from hilltop, or Lil Opry
stage, instead, the melody comes
in crisp on the edges of faint
radio from three counties over.

Wsike in harmonized, old-time
mandolin song lines. And sun
on elongating sycamore shadows,
hints at a flattening of earth.
Forest hill shadows resplendent
with electric modulated trills

Chihopèkëlisak dangle in wood
song and canter from chorus
to chorus. In these hills, along
these forest ridges, we settle.
Commonwealth moves north
and greets home with a chorale.

Swear that the forest ridges
themselves leak the medicine
of our holy father of bluegrass.
Through the static, scratching
at loose leaf underbelly earth,
picked at in chikënëm hwìkahsha

quarter steps and we reel about
through forest bottom, softly
in time with the departure of air
humid and still dense in wet leaf
aspirations to rise above and be
heard through the dense canopy.

And the song settles, these amplified
calls of long abandoned maikhatina
and these hills bristle, these hollers,
these fields of persimmon-sweet
ridges as distant porch lights ignite
through a coal vein darkness that
calls out home through every shadow.

Mpihpëntaok

at New Harmony, IN

Upriver the sisilieyòk forded
the Wabash.
Here it has always been
more quiet. Westerlies
kick up from the river
and ridges of trees hiss
between
shaxakwtis choruses.

From here Indiana spreads
north and east
and calls back
younger
with distance.

Utopia fizzled out here
in under two years.
the spark of a nascent
self-sense
a voice uttered between cabins
in the darkest forests beyond.

Closest to water,
nearest to ground
the Wabash whimpers
back a familiar line,
after a long listen I know
I have heard them before.

Hellbender at the Waterline

for wiinhkia (Cryptobranchus alleganiensis)

Know that our territories
inevitably touch. Every one
of them, us in the middle,
water washing away against
rocks, prone bodies, flowing
forever downhill, and us
in the middle unwanting
of touch but in passing.

To hold the middle point
is to uphold existence itself.

Names are often more
fierce than realities, and
shadows darting between
river rocks at twilight bring
the worst of mythologies.

The last of our water dragons
cling fast to the rocks swept
here by northern rivers, and
the waterline bends against
shadow as the dragons hunt
well out of sight, well out of
touch. Water flowing always
flowing and the middle held.

Blue Hole of Prairietown, Indiana

Our time stretches from places
that divide waters, from murmurs
of service station men, back through
levee breaches, where crust fractures
the waters run treasure state blue.

We place ourselves in relation
to water, admire the sun as it
bounces back, speak of that
which is lost to abysmal depths:
locomotives, lovers in a car,
playful children never returned.

Out of it too, rise warnings:
of hungry catfish, how outflow
wind turbine plate harmonics
poisons quietlike, the slow demise
of sweet cold water at the fringes
of our shared earth prophesize
that this kingdom of man ends
in fractured crust and shadow.

Perhaps mastodons fell in here.
As if this land received Tecumseh's
comet, the pit from which Harrison
drew rage to slaughter Lenape women
and children. Above this Vigo County
roadside know that it is quiet, spare
for the rapturous blackbirds and rustle
of cardboard-thick tall grasses. Know
what we put in far outweighs the sight
of that which myth carries beyond here.

All of Our Earth Drains to Here

at the confluence of the Ohio and Wabash Rivers

Uncertain, we pour
through sycamore fields
to lowland swells
the first lands
taken away. Osakame peoples

spreading north from south,
capillary action against
a darkness of forests
a buzz of prairie gnat
clouds. Heat and slow
drip of seasons, one calls
to keep the movement steady, water and
harmonies new and old at path's end.

The water down, the newcomers up
and that we held higher ground
for longer
means so little two centuries later.

That some remained, so few
that mythologies of our long demise
flow like tales of long-cleared forests,
and the surety of American progress.

Sunlight on water top
flickers like cat eyes
in a sunbeam.

To dissipate and return,
reform as nipënësak,
a darkened cloud alive
atop fresh sunlight,
warmed to frenetic wave riding,
and returned to forever sliding
water beneath us.

We shall swim upon waves
                    of radiating warmth
                    delivered by the sun
and revel in the motion of rivers.

Let us lie
          as if beside
          the Wabash

          Summer slanted
          outlined yellow,
          healing rests
          arrives like
                    a Chet Baker trumpet
                    low plaintive
gentle as the sunset
itself, marked
          by the idleness of water
          how it ambles south
          here
          is the point
          where the earth
          calls us to rest.
Willows hiss in the wind.
          and beneath the eddies
          of all our rivers meeting
          becoming one,
          the water ripples upward
          enough to tell us
this is not ours alone.

Divining Manëtuwàk at the Banks of the Wabash

Pick the dirt-mounded field
or fallow one of half-mowed
lawn and scraggly huckleberry
trees. Alongside old 67, let rest
the car upon the lip of grass,
loose gravel lining the path north.

Hold tight to this Y of a xaxakw
branch, walk straight line
from the car, slow, atop rain
hungry earth, hopeful in footfall,
moves that steadies; nehëniltipasèt
circling creation atop thermals.

Somewhere mid-stride, perhaps
at the windbreak ash bank
at field's edge, feel the manëtu
heavy in water churn, topple
downward the branch, feel its
demand to touch darkness below.

Drop to your knees, and dig,
fingers, nails through shallow
roots of imported grasses, peel
back the earth, till you breach
the outer walls of Cahokia, lower
still until earth itself is water.

In cold water, electric fingertips
feel manëtu flow through your
down-turned arms between earth
itself and the warmth of you against
a still climbing sun. Rest. Breathe
deeply of ancestors. Speak of returns.

Persimmon Ridge Greets the Day

Sing it like brilliant wetënteis
in a Morgan County hilltop
xaxakw. From here the world
merely slides downward, here
alongside sweeps of power lines
and the clear cut of this cabin,
part studio part home for exiles,
a pew before all creation. Persimmon
ridge autumn song is the sweetest
you've heard since Mr. Rosewater
answered that volunteer fireman's
phone during peak high water
season in canal country. Each note
a lush spreading pool of color
in T.C. Steele workday canvas, let
it drop to quiet like a front porch
Whitcomb-Riley sweet tea. Here,
Indiana is everything. Here, day
is downgraded to broad streets
between that simple birdsong
and breaking waves of Michigan.

Kwëchkwiyok Hitkuk

Kaoxën has declared its hunger, in studio
Rafael Sanchez reports Henryville debris
is smeared across Indiana's soul, the trees
they are paintbrushes thick with tar oil,
ink for epitaphs about all that falls down,
Old Mac watches news in his parlour shelter.

Rafael Sanchez pleads for all to find shelter
rides calm as furious kèshxink batter studio
walls. He talks although the lines are down
and we know of many casualties, debris
strewn across interstates, rain heavy like oil,
liquid clouds dragging terror through trees.

And they moved, despite the night, trees
bent and released in wind spasms. Shelter
us all from state-long storm lines. Like oil
they spread, soul-cracking violence, studio
lights and toasted video replays, the debris
is all repeat, thuds of forests falling down.

Pèthakhuweyòk stomps through downed
utility poles. Raphael Sanchez warns of trees,
unsafe in their frailties, storms make debris
from centuries-old bodies, thrash our shelter
with those remains. Hunger pushes at studio
walls. Wind-wrapped rain clings like oil

to everything that it touches. Sanchez's oil
slick hair holds our centre together. Down
cast gaze at handwritten notes, the studio
lights dim as generators turn over. The trees
groan in unrelenting winds. Raphael's shelter
reflects in his glasses. Hints of failing debris

are ghosts in the transmission. Yet debris
is not the essence of our soul, time like oil
marks our passage here. It falls upon shelter
after shelter, sky slams stolen earth down.
Rain follows wind, seeps through the trees.
The end arrives in a darkened silent studio.

A Massacre of Mourners

for pankihtamw (Conuropsis carolinensis)

Consider this field,
open to the Seymour County
sun, ringing heat
at the wrong time of the year.

Call them by name,
pankihtamw,
into the windbreak,
pankihtamw,
as our Tuwèhtuweyok hosts
would call to them.

Starlings return their garble of birdsong.
And the wind from the nearby hilltop
is ceaseless. Urgent in its
northern
push.

They were easiest to kill
because they gathered
to mourn their dead

bewildered at the men
burning trees, bundles of feathers
the orchards and fields
the killings, the killings,
and the killings.
to own the land
was never enough.

And the willows
the red buds
the catalpas
are restless
and the starlings anxious
skirt at a murmuration

not one willing
to put claw to killing field,
the old field, the crooked
faltering barn and house

mourner and murder
long returned to earth
and the hungry farm with them.
And the starlings are in flight
like a descending sheet
above the golden rod and thistle.

And the earth is hard
and quiet
and lifeless
in the hue
of a still
setting
sun.

MËKËKÈKINK

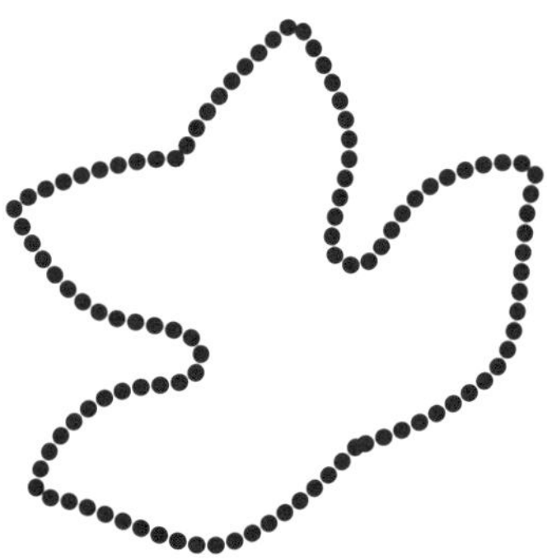

Hard Plates Break the Surface at Fulk's Lake, Indiana

for the Beast of Busco

The backwash flows through Clark Chapman Ditch,
doglegs before it nears the Churubusco town line,
folding under farm fields and woodlots. Listen, field
sparrows mime each other from cabins across the shadows,
mimicking questions of who's there and exactly why.

And the pond, the waters are still. Yet the surface vibrates
with tension and hunger and motion of nearly a hundred
thousand bodies. Did the old ones mention this anxiety
in the quiet? And I am left to search the pond for breaks
in the stillness. Because pamputis rose up to catch our
falling sisters. And the water is still with pressure upon it.

Myths rarely rise, even less so on demand. Yet, my urge
is to demand. When every saviour since that first shell
failed us in ways worse than death, we must fall back
upon what is known. Once pamputis caught us in our
fall. And few if any relations walk this Maumee land.

The pond was drained. All his Life magazine photos
were useless. And then all the land left to refill, and us
all to consider the improbability of a half-ton turtle
in a small pond near the dried-out body of the Maumee
river valley. No matter how grand and righteous our
demand, the silence and still waters will answer us back.

Opèk Sipu Catches Sun Before It Flows Beneath the Washington Street Bridge

Know that Creator caresses this land
around us with each sun rise, and rivers
move against these eroded contours,
glide between the worlds we construct
out of fancy for the things we need
to be and the gifts bestowed upon us.
These waters before us emerged
from a Randolph County farm field,
draw in suburban silt, rural wastewater,
urban detritus, dance in the warm
runoff of a persistent heartland sun.

Where the white sand river meets
unsteady shore Doc Ward received
the Walum Olum sold it to a nascent
colonial nation that knew only rumors
of yakweha battles, the gifts of crows,
how creation comes into being through
the sacrifices of muskrats. Listen here,
in the murmur of perpetual water motion,
to how prophets sing the world back
from the cataclysms of shaking earth,
meteors returning to earth, midday all-
encompassing darkness. Our Indiana
home is built upon the scaffolding
of a hundred thousand stories, each true,
each spun by wood-turning calloused
hands, each carried through a multitude
of individual migrations, concludes
in naming a portion of creation home.

Above gossamer fishing lines
cast to river body, searching out
wisamèkok and shëwanamèkw, US
40 rattles east to west through
this state, through this city at its core,

and before the bridge overhead
kishux draws the water, honeycombs
a cadence of slow peeling medicine
we need sung into the promises
issued before spectacle races
and the sunrises we understand
Kishelëmùkònk grants us each day.

Massacre of Indians outside Marshville, IN

"In 1824, nine Indians were murdered by white men near this spot. The men were tried, found guilty and hanged. It was the first execution of white men for killing Indians."

Sign, cut from cornfields
rustic like the jaw line
on an Adams Township
old timer, assigns blame
for a brutality rooted
in external fears turned
to rage, wars that shall
not end. Declares that
some of us are murderers
of the wrong sort. Ease
of prairie winds against
fresh white farmhouses,
corn bent to wind, sign
and homes defiant in
different ways. Simple
hard-jawed signs repeat,
time settles around us
onto land that holds blue
sky up, yet retains bones
from nine people and some
murderers that killed them here.

Respite Along the Place Where the Water is Roaring

Standing at Ceenkwihtanonki

Know that it roars and
the shore here is blessed
          and the skyline of the city
          stretches her unfolding arms
to the heavens,
          replicating Lady Victory
          holding the south at bay.

Look upon the waters
          churning bottom
          falling   between   river
                    rocks   that   White Eyes
himself   must   have   drawn
                                                  cold water from.

And the persistent sound,
          of water hollering
          under the purpling sky.

Waters are more loud than violent
          posturing among driftwood.

Upriver the waters are slow,
          arching in a slow descent
          from an indiscernible summit.
To begin as trickle
          every downgrade in earth.

And the volume is surely celebration.

From here,
          that upland
          is a rumor more
than a place.

Wapicamicoke   Wapeminskink

Strawtown   Killibuck's Village

And the crush of water and stone
carries those words, silt and soil
covered through the hills and hollers
to the south,
surging backwards
to a Commonwealth
of cranberries and fallen grandparents.

Nënëmhùkwe, they roar
because water
and spirit
only slumber,
and the gouged out
forests have lost
their voices
to townships,
sprawl of what
was once to come
next.

Witke Kitutènay

for Ann Dancing Sculpture, Ceenkwihtanonki/Indianapolis, IN

Ann, sway sweet through dusk,
arms braced, ceaseless gentle caress
of implied hips against darkness,
bare electric arms swaying, whisk
sweet cream neon legs, corn husk
dress she beguiles this city in dance.
Ann, sway sweet through dusk,
arms braced, ceaseless gentle caress
this kitutènay of sober rest, awaken
these ascetic cross streets. Seesaw
with her, us all pitukëna in dulcet
breeze, hushed paean of time taken.
Ann, sway sweet through dusk.

Audubon Grass Dance

Ornamental grass shakes
            alongside Audubon
            one-time laundry mat
selling hipsters umbrellas
            to a full house
                        empty parking lots.

For a moment I believe
            Lincoln's ghost train
            couldn't cross the path
beyond. That Irvington
            dreamed itself up
            a Carmel. We rest

in this eastside island
            build upon two generations
            of gentrification, consider
            the chaos of speedways,
            fluid rush of commute times
            and the steadiness
            of swaying grass beneath
            the Washington Irving bust
            in steady prairie breeze.

Outskirts

for Eleanor

Call the water as it bends
Consider that you are falling
backwards, a flutter of vertigo
as if you tip back your chin
too quick, catch yourself
as your daughter laughs.

The shifting between worlds,

here at the high-lofted barn
risen against the outskirts
of the first neighbourhoods
you called home in the lands
your ancestors walked,
    never spoke of later,
    recite this feeling
    aloud, drunk on
    quick movements
    along worn wood
    hardtop dancefloor
all as memory act on this land
    of exile. Tell her

this is hers. She will know
of Indiana through an Edison
bulb barn dance, the way it
    can sing of cranes
        soft foot walking
        upon farm fields
        and leads you along
        the forested hill tops
of Persimmon Ridge,
    alive with bluebird song.

Outside, through heavy autumn
air, lights burn back through

even horizon of the wind breaks,
the expanse of Naptown beyond,
              and the memory maintained
              is song, soft light, smoothed
wood of the barn floor, whirl
              of several cotton dresses
              in the bronze dim light.

When the slight spin, flutter ends,
vertigo and the night find you
                            in a rented living room
with a distant rumble of airplanes
returning to earth, and the light
autumn rain misting the dug-up
fields beyond, the hope stands that
here too will be the place she recalls
Indiana as the place where worlds latch.

A Reflection of Sky

Begin with upward gaze
    and follow
        the light
        as it arises lucid
    in these latitudes,

with the shallow gurgle
        & drift,
                Ànkòhëna Sipu,
            she slides past
    sycamore shore beds,
                    past
    kitutènay steel and kitutènay glass and kitutènay concrete

Upon her
    to see the sky
    opened sky
        and lazy clouds.
    Over land
    that once made
    us call out
    disheveled pleas
    into the shadows
    and hills between
    cabins and traces.

Fractals of determined
sunlight   &   water
    atop sweet earth.

We are a reflection
    of sky. And
    it is
    the
    deadly
    season

where it's all dried out
plants,
            yellow patients,
past ripe fruit
dried tufts
of bird feathers

Ànkòhëna Sipu Snakes Past Columbus and We Are Pulled Forever West.

for Aankwaahsakwa Siipiiwi/East Fork of the White River

Eastern Fork of the sacred river
is claimed
to begin
due south
of Columbus.

Here, Driftwood becomes White River
and the reclaimed water runs
south and east, meeting
hellbenders and sing-song
cascades passed between
long abandoned cabins.

Even here the state runs back
to the furthest corner
of the world, drawing
all the waters with it.

Our gaze held east
our motion slides us west
and slightly
south.

Drift near the bridge,
this beautiful bridge over
the sleepy waters below,
and night-lit cable stays
drift by becoming strands
of internet web satellites
indiscernible from the clutter
of junk between us and where crow
flew up to save us all.

And drift, leaf
upon oil sheen river top
the ancestors above,

the words, porch lights, broken leg
        hum and grumble of the interstate
        hapless above and stretched out.

They have no pull. Look north
                to the height of the world
                beyond the treetops
                and pockmark subdivisions.

Somewhere beyond that point
          there will be …

until then. Rest. And river
                around us
                like a river
        that knows nothing of northern promises
                may draw us down
                        to the shore again
                        and we witness
                        that leaf follow
                        the contours of
                        the earth south
                        of us.

Èhènta Wehikiyànkw

Nearer sunset, sky nearly matches
                    the orange, yellow
                    of the Pilot Service
station overhang. And the trucks
migrate through as if lost herds.

                    Peterbilt   Penske
          Cummins   Gerth's Overland
                    Yellow
                              Penske   Penske
Harding Street filthy,
                    used up like an oil rag
                    jettisons heat back,
fever. endless noise. listless

our old homelands at the cloverleaf.
mèthakèxën, èhènta wehikiyànkw,

the herds push through
          dusk and
          the sun sets
          across the interstate
          pouring in rich dying
          light from the west
          and
to the south the land drops
into patchwork hills and hollers,
swallowing up Opek Sipu,
                    a murmur
                    between trees.

All of it ceaseless in the approaching night.

ANUKANINK

Ehëliwsikànk Nkiikàmaok Anukanink

John Hill recorded his passage
        through the west on rags.

Lenape being Lenape
        to move   with sisilieyòk   to the headwaters
                                                                        of
                                                                        the world.
        And the impossibility here of being sustained
                                        of those phantoms
                                        sun bleached burial mounds
                                        of trace makers, of life
without the hard property lines.

Record this passage,
                upon Moleskine waxed paper
                and those ghosts live on
                without sustenance.

Sikòn nurtured plains of mud,
                        overrun rivers, petrol springs,
                        this place at a far radial
                        arm of where land
                        slides away from Muncie.

Here the phantoms control the margins.

Across wide-skied Interstate
                forlorn sun that cooks water
                and earth into slurry and the scent
                of an old man breathing hard stories
                onto you.

No Eagle boy awaits the wars that lay ahead.
        In his place, the defiant winds howl
                        across muck fields and lost grave markers
at the edges of Springfield,
        in the slipstream

        the air draws
        the entirety of the settlement
                in closer
circle k, subway, and shell of a long-closed Mart.

Here there is only mud
        and there is sky
        and the memories
of hardened tears, long-forced marches
and hope that Eagle Boy could
        appear on the horizon
                if only to show us the way out.

Sikòni Maehëlan

We are greeted by the first dog
    holding guard at the western way.
    Follows us the length
    of the set-back drive,
    pops
        of   gravel
    tire to tire to underbelly.
He ambles alongside until we rest
among the jumble of old cars, fallow
    garden containers.

Gathering at the furthest edges
        of familiar land,
        the middle west.
Gathered in the mire of last season
        and the hope of next.
And the radio is off, and gravel loud.
    What is dry enough to move
    is unsettled enough to growl.

In the lands of great Indian Killer,
    a father of war cloaked
    in lawyer robes and backwoods
        swagger of a man who kills
        sisilieyòk because the people
    call the act good and fair.

The mud from the last week's storms
            clings to the fur
            of that first dog.
Harold left the dog and the farm
years before we stumbled east.

Beyond is the rise of trees,
    the old cabin his widow points out.
But the mud is too deep and so little is left.
    Even the smallest walks are misery
    near the riverbank.

And the dog, that first dog,
                this last dog,
        sniffs us over, accepts small affections,
and returns
        to the dog house
        Harrold left him

and the sun through the willow thicket
        burns my eyes with prisms
                freed from the far western horizon.

And the crows call out from fields
        nearby, raspy warnings of new arrivals
        through the light, through the crunch
        of gravel, and musk of too much water.
This opens our gathering
                on
                        broken
                                        land.

Horseshoe on Rye

believe you me,
the weight of this plate
holds down this tavern
at the edge of Springfield,
close to I-55. The world
halts here. At the edges
the town is crumbling
to grit and section eight.
Type of place where no-
one is right or wrong,
and the silver nosed tomb
is the primary orbit
myths and hope follow.
What came from here,
feels long departed and
the earth is wet, malleable
in uncomfortable ways.
For river pirate cries and
Pottawatomi tears, earth
here is fertile if abused.
Horseshoe on thick rye,
a surprise beneath coat
of cheese sauce. Fries and
ham adhere to what is less
than natural. Know it works.
The centre holds, although
the edges, they are weak,
and the sauce is cooling
and the interstate traffic
won't stop and the wages
they won't budge, but
the sauce is near perfect
and it all gives under
tongue, and the sweet
and the smooth, the tang.
of all of it mixing in ways
neither right nor wrong.

These Sëpinko Currents

for the Sangamon River

All waters, like people
have fallen from the sky.

Overtime we fear
sound that drops
like
a
fox
snake
from
a
catalpa.

Worst things come
from above us
rarely beneath.

These are shallow waters
that pool up around black
dirt earth. Grass
carp feed upon
root tangles, filth,
wrestle life from
busted-up farm
earth. And it is
hardly clean fill
along this muddy
heavy
river.
What remains
smells of iron
and I think
on sëpinko,
how little there are by volume
but how they fill up everything.

The mild season is here.
After sorghum is down
ready to suck the sweetness
remaining from the earth.

Those waters
and the earth
and every drop of sun-
kissed sugars pulled up
from them, have rested
seven generations here.

There are so few here
to return sëpinko
to a diminishing river
to a muddy place
where Puteòtàm
crossed through darkest nights,
longest days, put down a deep trail
between homelands and exile,
through these silt-fed fields,
and sëpinko rendered from
another long, forced march
leaving death-drawn sugars
that find their heavy harvest
in the shallow, ever-flowing waters.

Mèlikën Kìkinhikàn, Ika Nta

at Lincoln's Memorial

To be hailed as warrior,
as emancipator
as Great Father
means what rests before me
in this repository of the dead,
in the city at the muddy edges
of everything is the lodestone
to hold mythologies together.

With ease, on foot, one understands what is absent.

Dakota 38
the lands
the lost relations
half-truths told
to build a nation,
we cannot count.
They have no place
in this tomb.

And the obelisk rises
like a sycamore wouldn't
above the cemetery
around us.
A tomb to build
better stories from.

Flanked by raging war ponies,
black to the soft limestone
backdrop, a headstone
to all things a nation
needed in man.

What rises to a still growing canopy
of shade trees holds the ground made
to tie a bloodlust and theft confederacy

into contradictions
of myth
of history
of suffering.

What remains of this man,
lies elsewhere
beneath it all,
in the granite
mausoleum
above
us.
A body visible resting
upon
and
into
stolen land.
And the statues and the man
all rest confident
that limestone
shouldn't fear water
and that time flows
like that river.

And the waters of the Sangamon
push the soils, gravel beneath us.

Know that in Irvington,
two hundred miles east
the train forever carries
him here. Light
across the prairies
and it peters out
by the shores of Opek Sipu.

Spirit light lost in time and distance
and the rails are arrow straight
through this muddy land,
run south of here and on
into an unfathomable West.

Here it is all said to rest.
And in the heavy stillness
of another spring in,
beneath convulsing
war ponies, he too finds
rest, this bronze man
          of Mèlikën
          peace dreams,
          trails of tears,
          scorched histories,
          cities, plains,
          shattered limbs.
Or at least the bust of the man
oversized and shiny-nosed,
                    he rests.

And there were visions of Prophetstown
          where evil men's heads rest on pikes
          and our women and children shelter
          away from them. Dreams. Unfillable.
          To rewrite that the comet predicted
          beginnings and not endings. Dreams.

And this here, this obelisk
                    this skyward
                    stab at immortality
          is a reckoning over a vision.
          I stand before another Indian Killer-in-Chief.
          more revered than reviled. Bust as oversized
as romances of any of peaceful white saviour.

Old ones would say to look at their nose
                    first, you can
          tell the mark
          wëshki left,
          how deep-rooted
their illness would be.

And his shines in the dullest light
of this spring morning. Everywhere
the sky threatens to fall, again.
And it shines from a hundred million
hands that rub at the myth
                    whose ghost train faded
                    outside Terre Haute.

Every motion misstep lands one here.
And skeletons carried are familiar
                    like
          creeks between licks,
                    cabins in hollers
axing swinging
                              men of morals.
Pursued as each of us is
          by how much we can bend truth
          to bring peace from a bloody story.
How the death of one gaunt lawyer
                              can cover
hundreds of thousands of other deaths
          because a tragedy is easier
          to come to grips with
          than genocide or fratricide.

Where the West is impossible from here
the South looks heavy like a filthy horizon.
          The musty ribcage beyond the furthest
          bank of trees, where even Abe
had to know was where it all began.

To move. And move. And move. Always to the North.
          Our nascent turmoil cools in the North.
          Reach upward, to the crackle
                              of northern stars.
I am thankful the obelisk is muted
by the walls of trees. Their stature is a refusal
                              to concede every last bit of light
                              to the Hoosier woodsman.

Restless
as the ones they chased
away building church halls,
strip malls &
judge pulpits,
from earth
turned tacky with blood,
tears of absence
& departures.

And where we rest,
is rarely where we fall
or come into this world.

But oh, that day when I find rest
may that ground be firm beneath me
and distances between closed
in dull afternoon light.

The Donner House

What starts here, in the white house
                    above
          the winding
                    road
                              outside
          Springfield.

And we are here
          in the worst grit
          of spring.
                    All heavy in shade,
everything runs cold and clings to you.

          In passing sun,
dust and dirt outline you
                              in aura
                    that grinds against skin.

The house is white, nearly grey
                              where sun
                                        hits the loose
                                                  siding boards.

Don't linger long enough
for phantoms to stare back.

The road south from the house on the hill
          goes on for only few miles
                    before the
                    Sangamon
                    bisects it.

West that road stretches on
                              to the prairie sun itself.
And we cut south,
          meet the river
          with its murky

    metal-heavy body
    that with its tired
          body
heaves against farm fields
and municipal drains
    carving with what little
    it still contains. And the sun
nestles closer to the tree tops,
    and closer yet to the horizon
          due west of here.

Firing .38s Alongside the Sangamon River

for Joyce McAfee

Question is never if the pie pan could take the shot. But rather what sort of violence the shrapnel can exhibit in flight. Dispersed into the air between us and the Illinois landscape, scattershot like the myths the river rats pull with them through the world. Even at distance, across trees, up the shore, and beside this atavistic settler homestead, one is certain you can hear them paddling upriver. Bullet torn aluminum beams back distress in an all too familiar way. Rattle. Flap in wind. Muted chatter down slope filters to us dappled in sunlight slivers that fall between catalpa leaves. Mhùkwinùnt, the blood-coloured ones, lurk in that same greenery. The water this season is nearly clear up through the back fields. Sipakònàk and muck clear to riverbank horizon. And the dead man's vintage cars still rest under the crooked gutters and busted back roof of the furthest shed. Perhaps this gun was his. The land never was. Although one may have coaxed fool-hearted belief of the second. She holds on despite. She holds his ground here. Hands me the freshly loaded pistol.

Depressed trigger shakes
blood-coloured ones from thickets.
Light. Sound. Flight.

KITUTÈNAY SHINKÀSKUNK

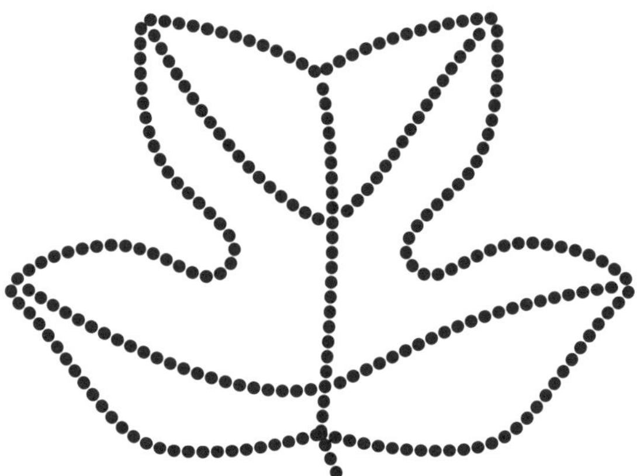

Kpaane

(i)

When you arrive
your thoughts will be full
of promises held by arrival.

All the routes north,
in spite of watershed
regardless of haunted
earth crossed, have led
to the land of fragrant
grasses, now reversed
waters, and high-rises.

We have seen this land
in Blackhawk fever
dreams. We have seen
the lake rise into
smears of light, metal,
rock stretched to horizon.

This arrival by air.

Midway opens before
me; stormy, husky,
brawling through cargo
train replica hallways
repainted white, grey
smudge undertones.

Turbo prop white noise
careening through my head,
repeated movements tracked
through print-out signs, arrows,
contraband warnings. Fear
which follows daring border
crossings. All departures,
unnatural and necessary.

Through unmentionable
security, and spelled out
above luggage belts, *Come*
and show me another city
with lifted head singing
so proud to be alive, all
white-teethed women,
laughter, the electric doors
past the customs booth
opens upon the fork tips
of a Sears Tower triumphant.

(ii)

When you arrive
the earth will embrace sky,
lay quiet on unsteady land.

L Trains above wooded
interstate intersections,
ahtu at the edges, ahtu
intermingled between
saplings and mattresses.
Fork tips atop skyline
and the lake beyond.
Everything here flows
towards Saint Louis
and being lake-bound
is striding counter current.

Oaks fill up the gaps
of sky between brick
craftsman, midcentury
apartment blocks, green
and resplendent with dew.
behind the corner
taquerias, xinkòhpukwès coat
glistens in morning light.

(iii)

When you arrive
phantoms of tipis will rise
above empty Wrigley Field.

We never left. No one
ever leaves.
And the ground
is unsteady like
muck
in
a
downpour
.

To live here is to rise
above ground. River
diverted means we
could find ourselves
floating the wrong
way, back south.

The stars are our ancestors
and they call to us, reach up.

They held the Nikes
at Michigan's shore
and threats arrived
from beat cops,
urban planners.

Indians don't belong
on rockets. Wrigley
your walls hold back
a multitude.

(iv)

When you arrive
Pure Michigan will cover
buildings, call across lake.

Above the Mobile Station
upon a rust brick multistory
folk art
proclaims purity
lies across
the lake,
in another
state.

And the soundtrack
is a crush of car tires
on perpetual motion
roads.

We never leave. Yet we do.
And the call across the lake
sings out in mèxkalaniat
rapture, like a call against
a wind-rippled flag, the song
sung over stolen land,
imported mythologies.

(v)

            When you arrive
kinglets will fill the trees,
and talk will be on heat.

Paulina Street oaks
vibrate with kinglet
steps and flutters.
Stopovers going
south, directions
are all wrong. We
            want but to head
            north, having come
            the bristle at anxiety
            of departures.

It is the heat
and it is the heat
and the trees
know this too.
But cannot move.

We are not ànkòhëna.
We are not kinglets.

But we are relations,
and our migration
            can never end
            in any other way
            than a prison.

Two Poets Discuss Migration and Ars Poetica over Pho at Lucky Pho 77, Chicago, Il.

a mediation on Kazim Ali and Hayden Carruth and Arrivals

Here, we are seated amongst
the vinyl and light of motion.
Reproductions, family photos
of temples, deltas, festivals,
left behind. Surrounded by
what one can carry, these walls
embrace a nationless home,
generations of departures,
generations of arrivals to come.
And that sun shines through
the Argyle Street immaculate
windows. We have come to rest.

Believe that the sweetest portion
of broth comes from that blue
of the lake nearby. Those waters
in constant commotion, free
in everywhere from time, naming,
borders, the exchange of goods.
We dwell and dine near the ether
that feeds dreams of promised lands.
Dreams racing from distant river
town sweet ramen through to this
inland sybaritic pho broth, we shuffle
chili oil spoons and oyster sauce in
patience, between all the words
that we understand to be stuck
in the mud of distant places, we
are men that carry ancestors closely,
listen to the whispers across myth,
across the borders we weren't meant
to cross. Nations are the lies we tell
to hold people in place, ensure
that economics and power favor
land thieves and their apologists.

Outside, through street-level
sunlight, dust and grease smoke
are eddies of a passing L train,
the horizon of our migrations
becomes a single whisp of grit
between buildings and cars.
Upward, outward, until it
dissolves into the light itself.
Once every train traversed
this big smoke. Walls shook
with each arrival, reverbed in
departures. A constant breath
from sisilias' moving ribcages,
the city one vibrating mass.
Land here knows nothing
of how we call it, the lines
we imagine upon earth. It holds
people tighter than postal codes,
notarized certificates, officially
endorsed births and lives.

Nearby chest freezer sings
luxurious in its electric hums,
akin to Fords clearing customs,
stop and go and stop and go,
a gunmetal calm of Fender
tube amp electric buzz, anxious,
awaiting the first strum of
rebellion, tradition, Jack White
electrifying the old to new.
And the wait is met with hum
of a billion particles moving
like a wave and they are sound
itself. Grand proclamations waft
from soup like water leaving the lake.
Nations and borders organize
wealth and power against those
same people they demand wave
their pretty multicoloured rags,
sing along to fairy tales of their

power. Poetics are song lines we
harvest from forced march tears,
melodies drowned out by thc borders
and the crush of our bodies against
them. *And to cross any border at all
means to submit one's body to the law.*

Here it is all mixing, and carrying
our worlds with us. Laws can search
our bodies, submission can only be
physical, and result is this northside
noodle house, at the terminus of
how we are meant to move upon
this land. Commonwealth in coaxed
from vinyl top tables, hardened
café tables, and plastic water cups.
Lucky Pho Number Seventy-Seven,
we are at the edges of the world
left to us, and we speak so little
of leaving, only of the broth
and the work that lies within us.

*We are all occupied by times
of war and the lust of invasions,
our natural places in the world
give up identities to steel and fire.*

His Russian Jew migrant folktales
of a Philadelphia awash with names
that Lenape ancestors left behind,
but never the bones of our dead.
What we still carry about are
chattel of uneven earth we've been
forced to traverse. Between water
glass refills, we worry about losing
this all to steel and fire, as so many
of us have lost before. And we know
that we are conditioned to object
notions of what lies beneath us,
what fills our lungs, and

Let us transcend
            the objective
                        world,
            including our
            conditioned
            egos,
and become a
            free,
            undetermined sensibility
in communion
            with others
equally free
and undetermined.

This is how two poets cross borders:
body first, driven by hunger, and pause
to watch over where we've come to rest.
We wear the marks of these crossings
through the whims of our desires,
the cravings for where we can never
pass again, the luxuries we never had.
We are the end results of our ancestors'
marches. Clock radio dân ca melodies
familiar as Wabash River sunsets, and
we agree that life and land is more
than organizing power and wealth
against those without. Allegiances
are often false relations to fictional
freedoms, and hot pot of water, fat,
and the pungent fauna of our land,
all of our land, is the sole embrace
that awaits us at the ends of our walks.

The lifetime of these rekindled
memory bursts in this daylight
noodle house beneath the L tracks,
and the songs we shall recount
are road songs, railyard blues,
and the steady rhythm of feet
upon soil and resounding even

beat declaring the steel and fire
shall not consume us, borders
are shame holdovers for laws
that keep us our each other,
ourselves, and the futures we hold

Hussain Recites Ginsberg While Driving Down Kedzie

Let the sour dampness of this autumn
    night fall into the shell of this rideshare.
    That the dampness of entangled worlds
    collect in unaccelerated air. Open it

with the hesitant chatter of men moving
    between nations, calling clans,
    pathways to names, how one trades
    time for money. In the passing

of storefront signs, traffic between
    neighbourhoods, the seamlessness
    of a city stitched together through
    knowing this to be the static center.

Hussain is our new millennium surgeon synching
    Ravenswood to Logan Park to Uptown.
    Across from a Vienna Beef dog retaining wall,
    he pauses, glides his sedan to a stop, proclaims

incomparable blind streets of shuddering cloud
    and lightning in the mind leap towards
    poles of Canada & Patterson, illuminating all
    the motionless world of Time between.

The streets before us, his sedan, all beef hotdogs,
    his voice, an intertribal rhapsody drawing
    together where we've been, what we've been
    called, releases them, free, into the city's night air.

Autumn Comes to Logan Square

Bring forth fall,
broken tree
and full of threat
we attribute to sinking leaves,
the passage
of another year.

Logan as it wraps
half around this eagle
topped park,
and housed by Milwaukee
stately into a dark grey,

dead leaves

three days pooled
on half-wet sidewalks
mirrors of passing showers,

it catches
the light
of dinner time
restaurants, cafes,
taverns.

Wits cleared,
gaze inward
from the sheets all too soon
approved of a Chicago winter.
Disappointment sings and in quiet
beneath the song of a bar jukebox
from the Cubs bar before us.
Know that a summer and spring
of repetitive dramas brought us
here, on the sidewalk before
a bar of dejected people finding
night warriors. We shall all greet

winter with the defiant posture
of White Eye's children, filled with
every hope that tavern signs, backlit
window fronts will get us through
            the next season,
                        and maybe beyond.

They Circle Above like Ravens

They circle
    like a thousand
    thoughts about
    how three story
    walk-ups, here
    on the gem of lake,
    is the promise land.

Air here is heavy with people
    and the way we recreate the world
    in our worst likenesses.

The planes come
    into O'Hare
    over the village tops,

from wood back deck of the third story walk-up.
    Their lights and logos are visible
    and reflect the settling sun.

Our word for raven
        is the same as lion
        "one who likes meat"
        winkeòhkwèt

And I have watched them
        torment the sky
        from an old port
        granary in a distant
        watershed.

I listen,
    almost watching
    ads and film clips
    from mid-century,
    Black   White   American
futurisms.

They are the ones that like meat
                        and they are circling.
            interrupted only by three-minute
            bursts of ads, pillows, cholesterol
            drugs, tile specials at Menards.

and the ads roll on
            longer than the credits.
            they circle
            and the promised north city
            exhales around us.

Union Pacific North to Lake Forest

I am to be collected at Ravenswood
            then
north from here,
            through to where
            the water is said
            to be sweetest,
            the forests thick
            like manicured
            edges of parade
            grounds.

            And the rail lines
draw on to the horizon,
            maybe east,
            perhaps west,
the city is a compass
            unto itself.

The way north,
our way north
            and the Union Pacific North.
            runs both ways hourly

Indeed, the sun is more golden
            and the brick stone station
            clean like a suburban Kroger

And when it arrives, the crush
                        the heat
                        the crush
            chases the starlings,
            but not the pigeons.

Cars of bruised aluminum call back
                    unpeopled to automats
and the yellowed, thick windowed
world slides past. Samples of middle-

American prosperity, tastes of chain
stores in craftsman storefronts.
                                        and the trees
                                        and the cars
                                        and the arms
                                                  with red light
                                                  clatter, tumble
                              dry past the windows,
                              blur into stations.

with names like forests

          Winnetka,
                    Hubbard Woods,
                                                            Ravina,
Highwood

          Lake Forest.

                    An elevated train
through Sandburg's dream upon
fragrant grasses.
          and verdant forests
          and soft sand shores
          beyond.

And the time between trains
is idle, becomes the material
                    between stanzas
                    a single breath
                    in the cooling evening.

What awakens life from there
          is the dumb weight of steel upon earth
          the rush of air fleeing the arrival,
          the stale heat of a fifty-year-old engine.

As the sun comes to rest
in the unfathomable West,
  I shall wait on that south bound
  train with its fury and its hard diesel
  breath, to drag me south again.

It is impossible to know the distance
one can travel or the distances we've
come from. What is certain is the maps
    are all constant works in progress
    and fallible like any early draft.
The clatter and the wallop
of the land beneath us, reads
  like the finality of a folk tune
  sung back in low-light, lives
  called back to us, as we await
  the gentle rest of sleep

before we begin afresh at first light.

GLOSSARY OF TERMS

The following terms come primarily from the Unami Dialect of the Lenape language. Their inclusion in the work is a critical aspect of decolonization as it re-inserts this language, its unique cultural connections and connotations, and its sound back into a public usage. The other labelled terms are from the Myaamia-Peewaaia language, the first language of the lands that the Lenape came to inhabit in contemporary Indiana.

amimi/amimiyok – passenger pigeon(s) (*ul*)

aèsësàk – animals

ahanhùkwi nuhëma – my deceased great grandmother

ahchuwikee – among the hills

ahope – rich man; rich (does not originate in material wealth sense, but rather like strong coffee

(ahopëwe), where the spirit and essence of the liquid is "rich"

Ahopesipu – a transliteration of the Shawnee (traditional name) for the Ohio River. Means the good river in the sense of it being rich

ahtu(hw) – deer

ànkòhëna – driftwood

anukanink – muddy place

Ceenkwihtanonki *(Myaamia-Peewaaia language)* – Indianapolis. lit.: "Here there is a roaring river"

chihopèkëlis(ak) – bluebird(s) (*Sialia sialis*)

chikënëm – wild turkey (*Meleagris gallopavo*)

èhëliwsikakw – west

ehëliwsikànk – in the west

èhènta wehikiyànkw – at our old homeland

hwìkahsha – claws

Ika Nta – I go there

ìkalìchi – further away

kaòkche – black-crowned night heron (*Nycticorax nycticorax*)

kaoxën – cyclone; tornado (wind that knocks things down)

kèshxink – wind

kikayuyëmënaninka – our deceased ancestors or parents or forefathers

kìkinhikàn – grave marker

kishux – sun; moon; month

Kishelëmùkònk – Creator (occasionally the Christian God. Although not here)

kitutènay – large city

kpaane – when you arrive

kwëchkwiyok hitkuk – the trees moved

lenii – common

linkwehëleokàn – vision of spiritual nature

maehëlan – gathering; an assembly

maikhatin(a) – camp(s). *noun*

manëtu – spirit (but in the sense of a supernatural essence that is not human. A spirit being)

manëtuwàk – multiple spirits (as in above)

mëkëkèkink – on the prairie

Mèlikën – American (United States) citizen/person

mèthakèxën – where one road joins another

mèxkalaniat – red-tailed hawk (*Buteo jamaicensis*)

mhùkwinùnt – north cardinal (*Cardinalis cardinal*is); lit. "The blood-coloured one"

mpihpëntaok – I have heard them before

nehëniltipasèt – chicken hawk; can mean either red-tailed hawk (Buteo jamaicensis), sharp-shinned hawk (*Accipiter striatus*), or coopers hawk (*Astur cooperii*). In the instance of this poem, it is a sharp-shined hawk

nënëmhùkwe – he/she/it roars

nipënës(ak) – gnat(s); generic for small flying insects

nkata ktan – I want you to move

nkata kwsi – I want to move

nkiikàmaok – I visited them

nkikayuyëmënaninkahke – our deceased ancestors or parents or forefathers (etc..)

Opèk Sipu – Lenape name for Wapahani (*Myaamia-Peewaaia language*) or the White River in Central Indiana. One time homeland of the displaced Lenape until subsequent forced removals

Òsaohane – across the river

pamputis – snapping turtle (*Chelydra serpentina*)

pankihtamw *(Myaamia-Peewaaia language)* – Carolina Parakeet (*Conuropsis carolinensis*) – now extinct

Pèthakhuweyòk – thunder spirits; lightning

pitukëna – milkweed (*Asclepias syriaca* ; edible type)

Puteòtàm – Potawatomi citizen/person

sëpinko – teardrops

shaxakwtis – tree frog (*Dryophytes versicolor*)

shëwanamèkw – American shad (fish) (*Alosa sapidissima*)

shinkàskunk – in the swamp

Sikòni – in the spring

sipakònàk – corn stalks

sisilieyòk/sisilia – bison (pl) /bison (sing) (*Bison bison*)

wèhènchiopànk – east

welhik – good

wetënteis – scarlet tanager (*Piranga olivacea*)

wiinhkia (*Myaamia-Peewaaia language*) – hellbender salamander (*cryptobranchus alleganiensis*)

winkeòhkwèt – ravens; lions; (literally the ones that like meat)

witke – he/she/it dances with (NB: In Unami Lenape language there are no separate pronouns for "he" and "she" or for "his" and "her")

wisamèkok – catfish

wsike – sunset; the sun is setting

xaxakw – sycamore tree (*Platanus occidentalis*); buttonwood tree

xinkòhpukwès – rat
yakweha – mythological bear
yapei – on the river bank
yukwe ènta kishkwik – today

ACKNOWLEDGMENTS

The author would like to thank the Ontario Arts Council for their generous financial support of this work. Immeasurable depths of gratitude to the following magazines, anthologies, and editors for their support of my work on this project.

"Opèksipu Catches Sun Before It Flows Beneath the Washington Street Bridge" *Belt Magazine/INseperable: An Indiana Humanities Program*, May 2019.

"Persimmon Ridge Greets the Day" *Arc Poetry Magazine*, Issue 91, Spring 2020.

"Divining Manëtuwàk at the Banks of the Wabash" *Augur Magazine Issue 3.1*, Spring 2020.

"From Here Northward" *Qwerty Magazine*, Summer 2020.

"Outside Cincinnati" *Retirement Plan*, Issue 5, Spring 2021.

"Sweet Ramen at Main Strasse, Covington, KY." *Retirement Plan*, Issue 5, Spring 2021.

"Blue Hole of Prairietown, IN" Spotlight on Poetry, Parliamentary Library of Canada, 2022.

"The Train Above 6th Street" *Capilano Review*, 2022.

"Massacre of Indians outside Marshville, IN" *Great Lakes Review*, 2023.

"Hussain Recites Ginsberg While Driving Down Kedzie" *Event Magazine*, Fall 2023.